GEN. T. J. JACKSON

STONEWALL JACKSON,
and the Old Stonewall Brigade,

by
John Esten Cooke, *1830 - 1886*

EDITED BY

RICHARD BARKSDALE HARWELL

Port. 'illus.

CHARLOTTESVILLE, VIRGINIA
UNIVERSITY OF VIRGINIA PRESS
FOR
THE TRACY W. MCGREGOR LIBRARY

Univ. of Va.   c. 1954

And men shall tell their children,
Tho' all other memories fade,
That they fought with *Stonewall Jackson*
In the old "Stonewall Brigade!"

From "The Song of the Rebel"
By John Esten Cooke

This is the first separate printing of John Esten Cooke's
*Stonewall Jackson, and the Old
Stonewall Brigade*. The original text, even to its erratic
punctuation, has been followed except for the correction
of a few typographical errors.

CONTENTS

STONEWALL JACKSON
and the Old Stonewall Brigade

GREATEST of Generals is General Stonewall Jackson.

Or, if that be thought extravagant—great among the great is the man of Kernstown, Port Republic, and Cedar Mountain—the hero of the Shenandoah Valley.

He had made his great fame before I ever saw him—made it in that garden spot of all this land of lands, the Valley of Virginia—and I had followed his magnificent campaigns in the region so well known and dear to me, with deepest sympathy and admiration.

I never knew him by any other name than that which the brave and noble Bee bestowed on him when he said, "Yonder stands Jackson like a stone wall."[1]

1. In its first issue, September 13, 1862, *The Southern Illustrated News* told how General Barnard Elliott Bee of South Carolina christened Jackson "Stonewall" at the first battle of Manassas: "Gen. Bee rode up and down his line, encouraging his troops, by every thing that was dear to them, to stand up and repel the tide which threatened them with destruction. At last, his own brigade dwindled to a mere handful, with every field officer killed or disabled. He rode up to Gen. Jackson, and said, 'General, they are beating us back.' The reply was, 'Sir, we will give them the bayonet.' Gen. Bee immediately rallied the remnant of his brigade, and his last words to them were: 'There is Jackson standing like a stone wall. Let us determine to die here, and we will conquer. Follow me.' His men obeyed the call, and at the head of his column, the very moment when the battle was turning in our favor, he fell mortally wounded."

That name of "Stonewall" thenceforth clung to him, and never will leave him, while the grass grows and the water runs. It represents his character and genius in the popular mind, and will descend upon the pages of history, and to children's children, as the name by which he was baptized, in fire and blood, upon the hard-fought field of Manassas.

And now let me tell you where I saw him first: how he impressed me, and what an humble soldier of the great Southern army thinks of the famous General.

I write in no hero-worshipping spirit here or elsewhere, I assure you; for I am constitutionally incapable of worshipping any human being—even though he be a hero of the most approved description, and the utmost celebrity. My father told me once, with a smile, that "he did not like 'great men,' and always avoided them." His meaning doubtless was, that the native bent of his temperament not only made it impossible for him to

"Crook the pregnant hinges of the knee,
    That thrift might follow fawning"—

not only rendered it repugnant to his self-respect to seek out and pay court to any one, but even to *appear* to act the courtier, by joining the obsequious throng.

I think I was born with the same unfortunate trait. I never could court anybody. I never could stand hat in hand, awaiting the Olympian nod—or bend the back, or make profound obsequious obeisance before his

Lordship or his Celebrity. In fact I hate the courtier, and the hero-worshipper, in all his ways: He and myself are alien to each other, and sworn enemies.

And yet I have the faculty of reverence for real worth, largely developed. I never worshipped hero yet—but I take my hat off and bow low to a great and noble soul like Jackson. He is a true "soldier of the Cross" no less than the valiant leader of our armies—and in his person centre the most conspicuous virtues of the patriot and the Christian. They speak of his eccentricities, his awkardness, his shy odd ways, and many singularities. Let these be granted. There is beneath all this in the soul of the man, a grandeur and nobility, a childlike purity and gracious sweetness, mingled with the indomitable will, which make him what I call him—a real hero.

I have often pressed his honest hand, conversed with him in those tranquil unencumbered hours, when neither the annoyances of command, or the breath of battle, touched his serene brow. He was more than ever great and noble, then; when laying aside his public bearing, so to speak, with his sword, he appeared in all the native and unforced simplicity of his real character.

But to my sketch of that first meeting which I have referred to.

It was on the battle-field of Cold Harbor, June 27, 1862:—so much had he thought and fought and suffered—and so often triumphed—before I ever saw him!

I looked at him intently with singular interest—

such as I have felt in few human beings—and with much curiosity.

The appearance of the famous General Stonewall was not imposing. He wore that old sun-embrowned uniform once gray, which his men are so familiar with, and which has now become historic. To call it sun-embrowned is scarcely to describe, however, the extent of its discoloration. It was positively scorched by sun— had that dingy hue, the product of sun and rain, and contact with the ground which is so unmistakable. A soldier from Franklin street, in his fine new, braided uniform, would have scarcely deigned to glance at the wearer of such a coat, and would have elbowed its possessor from the pavement with extreme disdain; —but the men of the old Stonewall Brigade, loved that coat; and admired it, and its owner, more than all the holiday uniforms and holiday warriors in the world. The cap of the general matched the coat—if anything was still more faded. The sun had turned it quite yellow indeed, and it tilted over the wearer's forehead, so far as to make it necessary for him to raise his chin, in looking at you. He rode in his peculiar forward-leaning fashion, his old raw-boned sorrel, gaunt and grim—but like his master, careless of balls and tranquil in the loudest hurly burly of battle.

Moving about slowly and sucking a lemon (Yankee spoil, no doubt) the celebrated General Stonewall looked as little like a general as possible. There was nothing of the "pride, pomp, and circumstance of

glorious war" about him, as my outline sketch estab-
lishes. He had the air rather of a spectator than an
actor—and certainly no one would have taken him for
the idolized leader of a veteran army, then engaged
in the battle to decide the fate of the Confederate
Capital. His dispositions had been made—his corps
had closed in like an iron arm around the enemy—
and having led them into action, marching at their
head, on foot, like a simple captain, he now appeared
to await the result with entire calmness, almost with
an air of indifference, trusting to a higher Power—to
that Lord of hosts who had given him victory so often.

Such would have been the impression of a casual
observer. But a closer glance easily penetrated this
apparent tranquility and carelessness. The trust in
God, and utter reliance on His will was surely there—
but no apathetic calmness. The blaze of the eye
beneath the yellow cap was unmistakable—there plainly was a soul on fire with deep feeling, and the ardor
of battle. A slumbering volcano clearly burned beneath
that face so calm and collected—the fire of Ney or
Murat held in leash and waiting.

I spoke with him but once—his reply was prompt,
brief, in the well-known curt, peculiar tone of the
speaker—short and to the point—which is best described by saying that the words seemed curtailed of
their full sound—clipped off—and ejected as it were
from the lips. It was in a like tone that he said—when
the afternoon of June declined, and the battle was

still roaring with great fury—to a messenger from
one of his generals:

"Tell him—if the enemy stand at sunset—to press
them—with the bayonet!"

His Chief of Staff, Major Pendleton,[2] volunteered
to accompany the courier, and ensure the safe delivery
of the message—and all know the result. The enemy
were pressed with the bayonet, near that deep ditch
and abattis, of which the General next day said, "The
men who carried this, were soldiers indeed!"—pressed
by the old Stonewall Brigade and their brave comrades. They could not stand before the onslaught of
this terrible legion, trained and made veteran in
the campaigns of the Valley:—and the red-legged
Zouaves, whom I saw next day, lying thick as leaves on
the field where the charge was made, exhibited the
consequence of the General's order.

During this "wild charge" the famous leader was
nearby but busy at the batteries which were fighting
the heavy guns of the enemy, a half a mile away on the
hill above the road toward Grapevine Bridge. He is
said to have a passion for artillery, and to superintend
its handling whenever he has an opportunity; certainly he exhibited this weakness, on the occasion in question. He kept close to the batteries, in spite of a
tremendous fire from the enemy, and seemed to seek
the localities where the bolts fell thickest. The
opposing batteries were fought with the energy of

2. William Nelson Pendleton, later Lee's chief of artillery, contributed
notes for the second edition of Cooke's *The Life of Stonewall Jackson.*

despair; and hurled upon our lines and guns, an unceasing storm of shot and shell:—but as the fire grew hotter and hotter, as the enemy's position became more desperate, it seemed to interest the General more and more. He rode to the right or left,— between the guns,—to the front within their line of fire—but always with his air of utter calmness. "As calm as a May morning" scarcely conveys the idea. He advanced amid the screaming projectiles, making the air hideous with their discordant voices, amid plunging round shot, and bursting shells,—with the supreme indifference of one who felt that he bore a charmed life, and could not be harmed:—and no less that our cause must triumph. The bravest men become aroused, and excited at such moments;—but I saw no trace of any such emotion in the General's bearing. His countenance, as revealed, in the darkness, by the glare of the cannon flash,—as afterwards when, the enemy having retired, we advanced to his fire, kindled along the road—was immovable as before. The slumbering volcano was there, doubtless—but from the moment when I saw him first, when his corps had just gone in, and he sat upon a log, by the old Cold Harbor house, writing a dispatch—to the end of the battle, when the burning brushwood showed his face, I saw nothing but indomitable resolution and calmness.—I doubt not he was leaning upon a stronger arm than man's, and had left the event to the God of Battles.

I describe the great General as I saw him. I have never seen him strongly moved—though often in

13

action. There is, however, no room to doubt the fury of the volcano within him, when it once breaks forth. Those who have been with him upon such occasions, declare that he becomes the genius of battle incarnate. Let the moment of extreme peril come, when the foe is pressing him hard, and endeavoring to hem him in, and destroy him. From the calm, collected spectator, so to speak, he becomes the fiery leader. Passing like a thunderbolt along the front he is everywhere in the thickest of the fight, holding his lines steady, however galling the fire, and rallying his men to the charge where the danger is greatest and the pressure heaviest.

His men are fond of telling how he exposed himself at Slaughter Mountain and elsewhere, saying to no one *"Go* on!" but *"Come* on!" They describe to you, how the eye flashed, the cheek flushed hot, the voice so low and calm on ordinary occasions, rose to loud and strident tones, as it called like a clarion, to the charge. At such moments, they tell you, "Old Stonewall," as they call him, cannot be recognized. The ice has turned to fire, the tranquil bearing to devouring excitement; and he leads the onslaught with the fury of a tiger, rushing on his prey.

Wo to the enemy who has to deal with General Stonewall at such moments—they are as stubble before the fire. The "red right arm" is carrying out the deep scheme of the powerful brain, and the possibility of a failure never seems to cross his mind. All energies of soul and sense are combined and concentrated in the stubborn and unfaltering struggle:—the flag of the Republic must be borne aloft in triumph tho' the dearest and most precious blood of the Southern land be poured forth like water. He does not spare his own. Where the great cause takes his men, he leads. The humblest private risks no danger which is not shared by his Commander. To him the cause is all—worth many noble lives—and he is ready to lay down his own.

To follow General Stonewall at such moments is a thing to tell to children's children:—and the flush of remembered triumph will overspread the bronzed cheek of the veteran who tells the story. It was then the bayonet charge was made, and the foe, however obstinate, scattered to the winds. For when General Jackson charges with the bayonet, the hour has struck—the struggle is decided. The field may be strewn with the flower and pride of the whole South, but the red cross flag[3] is floating still.

> "Ah maiden! wait and watch and yearn
> For news of Stonewall's band;
> Ah, widow! read, with eyes that burn
> That ring upon thy hand!
> Ah wife! sew on, pray on, hope on,

3. The "red cross flag" was, of course, the familiar battle flag of the Confederates. It was devised after First Manassas because the original Confederate national flag was confused with the United States flag. The battle flag was incorporated into the second and third Confederate national flags (1863 and 1865) as a union.

Thy life shall not be all forlorn—
The foe had better ne'er been born,
Than get in Stonewall's way!"[4]

In these lines, found they say "on the body of a
sergeant of the Old Stonewall Brigade, at Winchester,"
speaks the spirit which animates Jackson's men:
especially that "Old Stonewall Brigade," which, like
the "Tenth Legion" of Caesar, and the "Old Guard"
of Napoleon, has made its name forever famous in
all tide of time.

The Old Stonewall Brigade! What a host of
thoughts, memories and emotions do these words
excite! How like a call to the charge sounds the
simple mention of the famous band! These veterans
have fought and bled and conquered on so many
battle-fields, that memory grows weary almost of recalling their glories. Gathering around Jackson in
the old days of Patterson in the Valley, when Stuart
had but a handful of cavalry to watch the whole
border, and Ashby, our dead hero, was a simple captain—they held in check an enemy twenty times their
number, and were moulded by the hand of their

4. "Stonewall Jackson's Way" was written by John Williamson Palmer
within the sound of the firing at Antietam. Dated "Martinsburg, Sept.
13th, 1862," it was actually first printed in Baltimore; the Martinsburg
dateline was used to protect the identities of the author and publisher.
Palmer was a Southern correspondent of the *New York Times* at the
beginning of the War, later wrote for the *New York Tribune*, and finished
his wartime career in the Confederate Army as a member of General
J. C. Breckinridge's staff. "Stonewall Jackson's Way" was printed in many
Confederate periodicals. It was issued as sheet music in Richmond in
1863 by J. W. Randolph.

Gen. T. J. Jackson considering dispatches - at the Old Church near Mechanicsville Louisa Co. Va. Tuesday July 29th 1862
Drawn by Hon A. R. Boteler

great leader into that stern phalanx which no bayonet
could break, and no odds intimidate. They were boys
and old men, the humblest of the sons of toil, and
the flower of the land—but united, trained and looking with supreme confidence to their Commander.

And then commenced their long career of glory—
their wonderful marches over thousands of miles
—their incessant combats against odds that seemed
overpowering—their contempt of snow and rain, and
cold and hunger, and want of rest. The soul of their
leader seemed to have entered into every breast—
and "Stonewall's Band" became the terror of the
enemy. To meet that enemy, was to conquer him, it
might almost be said, so obstinately did the eagles
of victory continue to perch upon the old battle-flag.
The laws of the human body seemed to have been
reversed for these men. They marched, and fought,
and triumphed, like war machines which felt no
need of rest, or food, or sleep.

In one day they marched from Harper's Ferry to
Strasburg, nearly fifty miles. On the advance to
Romney they walked—many without shoes—over roads
so slippery with ice that men were falling and their
guns going off all along the column—and at night lay
down, without blankets, on the snow, with no camp
fires and no food.

At the first great battle of Manassas they were
nearly starved, but fought with desperation. At the
last battles there I saw them by the road side, where
they had halted, and one of my friends, a brave

17

young officer of the command, thanked me for a biscuit.

The very rapidity of their marches separates them from all soldier comforts—often from their very blankets, however cold the weather; and any other troops but these and their Southern comrades would long since have mutinied and demanded bread and rest. But the shadow of disaffection never flitted over forehead in that command. Whatever discontent may be felt at times at the want of attention on the part of subordinate officers to their necessities, the "long roll" has only to be beaten—they have only to see the man in the old faded uniform appear, and hunger, cold, fatigue are forgotten. The Old Brigade is ready—"Here!" is the answer to the roll call, all along the line:—and tho' the eye is dull from want of food and rest, the arm is strong and the bayonet is sharp and bright. Before those bayonets no foe shall stand—to pass them, is to advance over the bodies of dead heroes, grasping still the trusty musket, even in death.

Here is the song again of the sergeant, dead at Winchester—its rough music is inspiring:

> "He's in the saddle now! Fall in!
> Steady—the whole brigade!
> Hill's at the ford, cut off! We'll win
> His way out—ball and blade.
> What matter if our shoes are worn!
> What matter if our feet are torn!

'Quick-step—we're with him before dawn!'
That's 'Stonewall Jackson's way.'

"The sun's bright lances rout the mists
Of morning, and, by George,
There's Longstreet struggling in the lists,
Hemmed in an ugly gorge.
Pope and his Yankees whipped before.
'Bay'net and grape!' Hear Stonewall roar,
'Charge, Stuart! Pay off Ashby's score
In 'Stonewall Jackson's way!' "

The campaigns of the Valley; the great flank movement on the Chickahominy; the masterly advance
upon Manassas in the rear of Pope—these are the
fadeless glories of the Old Brigade. Their path has
been strewed all over with battles. Incredible have
been their marches; countless their combats—almost
always against overpowering numbers. The scythe of
death has mown down whole ranks of them; but the
Old Brigade still marches on, and fights and conquers.
The war-worn veterans still confront the foe, though
the thinned ranks tell the tale of their glories and their
losses. Many brave souls have poured out their blood
and fallen—but they are conquerors, and more than
conquerors, in the world's great eye. The comrades
of these heroes hold their memories sacred, and have
offered bloody sacrifices to their names. "Steady!
Close up!" were the last words echoing in the dying
ears—and the aim of the survivors was only more
steady, the charge with the bayonet more deadly.

Those survivors may be pardoned if they tell their children, when the war is ended, that they fought under Jackson, in the "Old Stonewall Brigade." They may be pardoned even if they boast of their exploits— their wonderful marches—their constant and desperate combats—the skill and nerve which snatched victory from the jaws of defeat, and, even when they were retiring before overwhelming numbers, made it truly better that the foe had "ne'er been born" than meet their bayonet charge.

In speaking of this veteran legion, "praise is virtue." Their history is blazoned all over with glory. They are "happy names, beloved children"—the favorites of fame, if not of fortune. In their dingy uniforms, lying stretched beneath the pines, or by the roadside, they are the mark of many eyes which see them not— the absorbing thought in the breast of beauty, and the idols of the popular heart. In line before the enemy, with their bristling bayonets, they are the terror of the foe, and the life-guard of their dear old mother, Virginia.

The heart that does not thrill at sight of the worn veterans, is cold indeed. To him who writes, they present a spectacle noble and heroic; and their old tattered, ball-pierced flag is the sacred ensign of liberty.

Their history and all about them is familiar to me. I have seen them going into action—after fighting four battles in five days—with the regularity and well-dressed front of holiday soldiers on parade. There was no straggling, no lagging—every man stood at his work, and advanced with the steady tramp of the true soldier. The ranks were thin, and the faces travel-worn, but the old flag floated in the winds of the Potomac as defiantly as on the banks of the Shenandoah. That bullet-torn ensign might have been written all over, on both sides, with the names of battles—and the list have, then, been incomplete. Manassas, Winchester, Kernstown, Front Royal, Port Republic, Cold Harbour, Malvern Hill, Slaughter Mountain, Bristow Station, Groveton—Ox Hill, Sharpsburg, Fredericksburg were to follow. And these were but the larger names upon the roll of their glory. The numberless engagements of minor character are omitted —but in these I have mentioned they appear to the world, and sufficiently vindicate their claim to the title of heroes.

I seemed to see those great names, as the Old Brigade advanced that day; and my whole heart went to greet them. Every heart that is true to our great cause, and loves its defenders, will do as much.

For these men of the Old Stonewall Brigade have been brave among the bravest—with their noble comrades of Gen. Jackson's corps, they have turned the tide of battle upon many hard fought fields.

They have "done well for the Republic"—and let their names be honored. Let the public salutation greet them—salutation by the lip and pen, no less than by the heart—meet them and greet them, and call them glorious—children of glory marching on to the Pantheon of Fame, in a great and peaceful land!

PART 2

See how I wander from the great commander to his men—from Stonewall Jackson to the Old Stonewall Brigade.

There are those who will regard my words as extravagant. I think I am only just. Let history, impartial, deliberate—summing up events, and weighing men and things in the balance—decide. The Old Brigade was fashioned and made effective by the hand of its commander—partakes of his own determined character —and will descend to posterity, on the pages of our annals, linked together with the name and fame of the great General.

Of this eminent man I have still some words to add. — Some details are necessary to complete my sketch: to show him, as he is, not only the idol of the popular heart, but the military leader of masterly genius, trusted and confided in to an unlimited extent by the great Commander-in-Chief of our armies.

That he is the favorite of his soldiers and the people, the very tone in which they speak of him will show. The crowd always jests with its hero, and magnifies his peculiarities. It delights to bestow nicknames upon distinguished men—as "Old Noll," "The Little Corporal," "Light Horse Harry," "Jeb" Stuart. His soldiers call Jackson "Old Jack," and "Stonewall"

23

—but generally the former. Innumerable are the jests, incessant the witticisms, which he inspires. The modest hero becomes a singular stage character thus; and without being humorous or witty, he is "the cause of wit in others."[5]

5. Attempting to recoup his fortunes after the close of war, Cooke sold a series, "Southern Generals in Outline," to the *New York Daily News* in the fall of 1865. His first sketch (published October 24) was of Jackson. Here he wrote: "Jackson had little humor. He was not sour or gloomy, nor did he look grimly upon 'fun' as something which a good Presbyterian should avoid. He was perfectly cheerful, liberal and rational in this as in everything, but he had *no ear* for humor, as some persons have none for music. A joke was a mysterious affair to him. Only when so very 'broad' and staring, that he who ran might read it, did humor of any sort strike Jackson. Even his thick coating of matter of fact was occasionally pierced, however. At Port Republic a soldier said to his companion: 'I wish these Yankees were in hell,' whereupon the other replied: 'I don't, for if they were old Jack would be within half a mile of them, with the Stonewall Brigade in front!' When this was told to Jackson, he is said to have burst into a hearty guffaw—most unusual of sounds upon the lips of the serious soldier. But such enjoyment of fun was rare with him . . . On one occasion only, to the knowledge of the present writer, did Jackson betray something like dry humor. It was at Harper's Ferry in September, 1862, just after the surrender of that place, and when General Lee was falling back upon Sharpsburg. Jackson was standing on the bridge over the Potomac when a courier, out of breath and seriously 'demoralized,' galloped up to him, and announced that McClellan was within an hour's march of the place with an enormous army. Jackson was conversing with a Federal officer at the moment, and did not seem to hear the courier, who repeated his message with every mark of agitation. Thereupon Jackson turned round and said: 'Has he any cattle with him?' The reply was that there were thousands. 'Well,' said Jackson with his dry smile, 'You can go. My men can whip any army that comes well provisioned.' Of wit, properly speaking, he had little. But, at times, his brief, wise, matter of fact sentences became epigrammatic. Dr. Hunter McGuire, his medical director, once gave him some whisky when he was wet and fatigued. Jackson made a wry face in swallowing it and Dr. McGuire asked if it was not good whisky. 'Oh, yes,' replied Jackson, 'I like liquor, the taste and the effect—*that's why I don't drink it.*' "

24

His cruel treatment of Gen. Banks, of New Orleans now, and the fate of that worthy's wagon trains, are well known. But the popular tendency toward humor is not satisfied until it makes General Stonewall declare that *"Banks is his commissary,"* and that *"he can whip any army that comes well provisioned!"*

He is silent, retiring, slow of speech, in consultations with his brother Generals. Hence the story that at Fredericksburg, during a consultation of this description with General Lee, General Longstreet, and others, he went to sleep and when aroused, and called on for his opinion, muttered dreamily, before he was well awake, *"Drive 'em into the river!"*

All his habits are scanned and magnified in this spirit of humorous exaggeration. He goes to bed, booted and spurred; he has buckets of icy water thrown over him *in puris naturalibus,* in front of his tent; he slaps his hand on his side as he rides; his lips are ever moving with ejaculatory prayer; — all these, and a thousand other stories are told of him, and ever repeated with additional coloring. — Any other person could lie down exhausted in his boots to sleep, or indulge in a shower-bath in the open air, or move his arms in riding, or murmur his prayers; but these things in General Stonewall Jackson are strange or comic, and become at once the food of popular stories. His soldiers cannot regard the individual or his character in any other light. He and his old sorrel horse—his old, faded coat, and sun-scorched cap— are inseparable in the popular mind. At Fredericksburg the General chanced to appear in a new suit of clothes—a fully decorated coat, the present of a brother General and friend; a superb, dark blue over-coat, and a cap brilliant with gold lace.[6] He passed along the lines, and soon afterwards one of the soldiers was overheard asking, "Where is Old Jack? Why don't he come on?" "Didn't you see him" replied the other. "Why, he passed by a quarter of an hour ago." The first speaker looked bewildered, and was evidently asking himself if General Jackson could possibly have passed by without his knowledge. Then he broke forth suddenly—"What! that fellow with the fine coat and cap? No sir! That wasn't Old Jack; it was somebody else!"

It cannot be denied that there is much in the worthy General to hang the hoops of a "good story" upon. He *is* unquestionably peculiar, original, and and *sui generis* in character and bearing. Nature has placed this pure and noble soul—this inexhaustible spirit of dauntless resolution, and heroic strength of will—in a frame which moves ungracefully, and would not appear to advantage in the haunts of the gay world. To quote the words of an intelligent observer: "General Jackson is not yet quite forty years old. He

6. "Children were also great favorites with him, and he seldom failed to make them love him. When at his headquarters below Fredericksburg, in 1863, he received a splendid new cap, gorgeous with a broad band of dazzling gold braid, which was greatly admired by a little curly haired child one day in his quarters. Thereupon Jackson drew her between his knees, ripped off the braid, and binding it around her curls, sent her away delighted." *Ibid.*

is of medium size and height—weighs about one
hundred and forty-five or fifty pounds—has dark, not
black, hair, and wears short side whiskers. His com-
plexion is rather pale, and his features, when at rest,
are destitute of expression. His manners are wholly
devoid of grace, especially among strangers, when
he is both awkward and embarrassed. On horse-
back his appearance is anything but prepossessing, as
it is almost under any circumstances; and one who
should meet him on the road, would be apt to take
him for a quiet farmer, with full barns at home, and
no creditor abroad, going to the Court House; or,
better still, for a country schoolmaster, who, though
all unused to the saddle, had undertaken to ride over
to a neighboring patron's house on Saturday, and was
meanwhile engaged in some difficult mathematical
calculation as he jogged along. But place him on
the battle-field—let the cannon begin to thunder, the
small arms to rattle, and the sabres to flash in the
sunlight—and the quiet farmer, the awkward, cal-
culating pedagogue, becomes a hero—calm and self-
possessed, it is true—but full of fire and energy,
quick as lightning, and terrible as the thunderbolt."

"Devoid of grace, awkward, embarrassed"—these
words describe strongly, if not with entire accuracy,
the bearing of the General. But the embarrassment
is rather a species of shyness—and this shyness of the
celebrated leader is not ungraceful; it has rather in
it something charming and attractive. His smile is
alone sufficient to redeem him. It is one of extra-

27

ordinary sweetness and kindness—so much so that
I think there was justice in the comment of a lady
who saw him, that "he had an angelic face."

But awkward or graceful, common-place or peculiar,
martial or pedagogic in appearance, the great leader
is the centre of all eyes and hearts whenever he moves
among the troops. He will live in song and story as
the popular hero of the war. Not more surely will
Stuart be remembered for his brilliant raids and romantic exploits with Southern cavalry, than Jackson
for his wonderful battles and victories with the men
who are known as his "Foot Cavalry." In spite of
the terrible marches which he has called upon them
to make, and which have procured for them this
nick-name, the General is adored by his troops. The
"Foot Cavalry" stick to their leader, and will not
believe that his equal exists.

Does a sound of distant cheering break upon the
air, a soldier standing by will say, *"There goes Jackson,
or a rabbit!"* The chase after a hare, or the appearance of General Stonewall, can alone excite that up-
roarious enthusiasm among the regiments. Go nearer,
and you will see a crowd on the side of the road, with
eager eyes, cheering; and the object of all this excitement will appear. It is an officer dressed in an old
faded uniform coat, with his cap in his hand, his
chin aloft, and his eyes nearly closed, who passes
at a gallop, with his staff strung along behind, also
uncovered, like their chief. The cheer will be taken
up, as the General gallops on—brigade after brigade

will echo it—until the sound grows indistinct—the depths of the pine woods swallow it—and the "Foot Cavalry" return to their camps or their bivouac, refreshed by a sight of their General.

I think that his men find graces and attractions in his very simplicity of dress and ways, in the utter absence of all pretension, or parade, or ostentation. It would be difficult to conceive of the leader of a great army corps more careless in his dress or his bearing. All the ways of the man are simple and earnest. He seems never to realize that any one observes him. On Monday, after the last battle of Manassas, near Chantilly, the enemy were advancing their cavalry and sharpshooters from Centreville, and the battle which occurred at a later period of the day, seemed about to commence, General Jackson was seated on the ground, leaning his back against a tree, and with chin depressed, and hands folded meekly on his breast—was fast asleep. I still recall clearly the simple attitude of the tired sleeper—the folded hands and the drooping head—and the spectacle was more interesting, to me at least, than that of all the richly clad generals at the great review I had seen the year before, for Prince Jerome, at Centreville.

I think that his troops feel toward him as I do—that they respect and love him for his genuine manhood—his purity, his simplicity, his unfaltering courage and deep piety. Did he fall asleep murmuring a prayer that day near Chantilly? I know not; but I saw him in the front afterwards, and there was no solicitude upon his brow.

If he prayed for victory, his prayer was answered. For at night the enemy were flying from Fairfax, and the second drama of Manassas was finished. The curtain had fallen upon the tragedy.

No man was ever freer from jealousy or envy than General Jackson. He never sickened at the laurels of another. On the contrary, he seems ever ready to discover and greet warmly the merits of his brother soldier, even though he himself is cast in the shade. This is no idle panegyric, but the truth of his character and temperament. He retains an unfaltering affection and admiration for General Beauregard, is on terms of the closest friendship with General Stuart, and his respect and regard for General Lee are unbounded.

"General Lee is *a phenomenon!*" are his words; and he added:

"I will go where they send me—under Ewell, or any one, if ordered—but *Lee I would follow blind-fold.*"

The words of Othello might be written upon General Jackson's tombstone as the motto of his life:

"It is *the cause,* my soul."

Another trait of his character has been much dwelt upon—what is called his "fatalism." It is said that his conduct in battle is the result of an Oriental fatalism which renders him insensible to fear. Many anecdotes are related of him, bearing upon this point. I have heard that while in Mexico, a battery was playing with tremendous power upon a road over which he desired his men to pass. They remained under cover of a bank, somewhat shaken in nerve, and unwilling to proceed in face of the terrible fire. This did not suit their commander, who did not seem to mind the firing, and walking out into the road, where the shot were plunging and the shells bursting, he quietly paced backward and forward, calling out coolly, "This is nothing—you see they can't hurt me!"

Another anecdote of a similar character will bear repetition. It was told me by a distinguished officer on the staff of one of our Generals, in the battles around Richmond. On Tuesday, in the hottest of the fight, he was sent with a dispatch to General Jackson. As he galloped toward the point where he expected to find him, the artillery fire grew so hot that it seemed impossible for any troops to withstand it. Trees were crashing down every instant, and the air was rendered sulphurous by exploding projectiles. He pressed on and finally was directed to General Jackson. He found him sitting on the side of the road, down which the enemy were pouring their most deadly fire—with round shot and shell ploughing the ground and bursting within a few feet of him—and this was the occupation of General Stonewall and General Hill, who sat beside him. They had a piece of bread each, and one bottle of molasses between them. First General Jackson would break off some bread, pour some molasses on it, and eat it—passing the bottle over to his companion, who did likewise. Then the bottle would be returned, and the same ceremony would be repeated. My informant says, the spectacle was the most extraordinary which he ever witnessed; and indelibly impressed upon his mind the conviction that General Jackson was wholly insensible to fear.

This insensibility is declared to be the result, as I have said, of a species of Eastern "fatalism"—such as the Mahometans sum up in the phrase "What will be, will be." The truth or falsity of the charge will depend upon the meaning attached to the term employed. Unquestionably General Jackson, and all men are fatalists in a certain popular sense—that is, he believes that *he will not die until his time comes!* But any other species of fatalism would be most absurdly attributed to him. For myself, I have no sort of doubt about his real sentiment on this subject. He is a devoted member of the Presbyterian Church— a church which has always embraced the doctrine of predestination, in its utmost scriptural latitude, and is no doubt strongly impressed with the truth of this tenet. Believing fervently in an overruling Providence, and trusting in the goodness of an omnipotent Creator, he gives himself no concern, except as to the performance of his duty. The issues of life and death are in a mightier hand than man's; and to that omnipotent power—to the "Sovereign Eternal Unchangeable Invisible"—he is content to leave the decision whether he shall live or die. What was the true and real

32

fatalism in Napoleon, is in Jackson, reliance on God. *Do your duty, and trust to Providence,* is the summary of the latter's religious philosophy—and that is better than trusting to the stars.

To a gentleman who exhorted him to refrain in future from exposing his person so greatly, General Jackson replied, "It has a good effect upon the men." Is not that the duty of a leader? — and if he fails in discharging that duty, is he culpable? I do not doubt at all that this eminent soldier strives, alone, to do his duty in the eyes of God and man; looking to no earthly crown, avoiding no peril, and leaning upon the promises, in the hottest hours of the deadliest encounter.

That is the "fatalism" of Jackson.

PART 3

It remains to speak briefly of General Jackson's
status as a leader of men—of his power to plan and to
execute military movements, with large bodies of
troops, in critical emergencies, and on a great arena.

I hazard my few words upon this point with un-
affected diffidence, for my entire want of all military
education in the schools renders any opinion of mine
of little value. — But perhaps I may presume, to
some extent, upon a practical acquaintance with
war in three or four campaigns, whose great actors
have passed before me, and in which I have been able
to measure, at least partially, the height of the
figures, and the qualities which go to round the
outline of the great soldier.

Beauregard appeared to me to be a born soldier
and leader when he dictated to Bonham that masterly
retreat from Fairfax to Bull Run, where the exulting
enemy ran blindly against the deadly hedge of Southern bayonets. Evans displayed hard-fighting faculties
at Leesburg, when he held the foe in check at
Edwards ferry, and closed in on them, with bullet
and bayonet, at Ball's Bluff, overwhelming and defeat-
ing them with his scanty numbers. Johnston
exhibited military faculties of the first order when
he held our lines at Centreville, in face of a powerful

35

enemy, with an army disorganized by inaction and reduced by leaves of absence—and when the enemy advanced, in front and on his flank, withdrew his command, and almost all his stores and baggage, beyond their reach. The repetition of the same movement in the Peninsula, when, completely deceiving General McClellan, he fell back from Yorktown behind the Chickahominy, was a new proof of his genius for strategy. Longstreet and Hood—*par nobili fratres*—and Hill, and others, acting in concert with their great companions, have many times made good their title to the first honors of the profession of arms, and at Manassas, Richmond, Groveton, Sharpsburg and Fredericksburg, held their ground with an obstinate and matchless daring which has thrown a fadeless lustre over their heroic names, and made them famous for all time in our annals. Of Stuart, the dashing cavalier, the daring chieftain, and romantic hero of the cavalry raid, who has reduced going round the enemy to a science, and originated with the hand of the master a whole new system of cavalry tactics—of this General the Yankee hordes whose communications he has cut, or whose trains he has captured, have borne unwilling testimony. Whoever has witnessed this leader at work, and noticed the manner in which he handles his command, will have discerned in his mingled dash and caution, the prudence and boldness combined, all the evidences of a native genius for war, and an aptitude for operating with the cavalry arm especially, which

fully entitle him both to the solid military reputation and the romantic fame which his career has
secured for him. Last of all—to end this hasty notice
of the brave spirits of the war—our great commander-
in-chief—first of living leaders, and second to few
in all time—has originated and executed the vastest
combinations, extending over hundreds of miles
of country, and exhibiting in their large proportions
and masterly details the hand of the spirit born to
command—to originate, to mature, to wait for the moment, and to strike with the power of the thunderbolt. Should General Lee be called away by his Maker
to-morrow, his great name and fame would live forever, and children's children would still repeat the
story of how he fell upon McClellan's right wing at
Richmond, and the rear of the boastful Pope at
Manassas—how, lastly, he foiled Burnside's advance
at Fredericksburg, and a third time put the foe to
ignominious rout.

With none of these great soldiers would I compare
General Stonewall Jackson. To institute such com-
parisons is invidious, ill-judged, and that General
would not fancy them, however flattering they might
be.

Let us try to estimate him without reference to
his great compeers, and solely by his military career.
The fate of many distinguished soldiers has been
his. *Colonel* Jackson of the early days of Patterson in
the Valley was acknowledged to be a hard man to
deal with at close quarters, and all that was necessary,

you were told, was a brain to think for him—a competent superior to plan his movements and tell him when to attack or retire. That opinion lasted for some time. Colonel Jackson could fight harder than any other man—was a veritable bull-dog indeed, and invaluable in his place—but he was in his proper place and should be kept there.

Then he fought his way to the command of a brigade. The old criticism followed him. *Brigadier General* Jackson was an excellent officer, had handled his command with distinguished success, but he had now, it was certain, touched his limit. A few regiments were not beyond his faculties, and his success with this "Stonewall Brigade," which people began to hear about, was unquestionable, but the command of a division was quite another thing, above all, of a division detached from the rest of the army, and constituting an army in itself. The responsibility would be far too great for the man; he could not safely be entrusted with *that* command. He *was* soon entrusted with it, however, and how he deported himself in his new sphere is well known. The critics began to discover that this eccentric, erratic Colonel Jackson had been misunderstood, underestimated, and when the appointment of Lieutenant-General was sent to him, they found it perfectly natural and proper.

In every sphere of action, and under ever-increasing command and responsibility, General Jackson had proved himself equal and more than equal, to the call upon his faculties; and the fashion of talking about his being "only a fighter" became, somehow obsolete.

The truth is that this great soldier has shone conspicuously wherever he has been placed. He was a good Colonel, a better Brigadier, and as Major and Lieutenant General has been best of all.

Let no spirit of partiality, no sentiment of admiration, dictate words of unmeaning panegyric, or a false estimate. General Jackson cannot be declared to possess the great powers of originating and combining which characterize the genius of General Lee. It is certain, at least, that he has never yet displayed them. But the presence of other great qualities in the man is unquestionable. His entire campaign against Banks in the lower Valley—the masterly manner in which he outgeneralled Shields and Fremont at Port Republic—the execution of the plans of General Lee on the Chickahominy and Rapidan—and the splendid manœuvring of his corps before Pope at Manassas, when he retired in face of the enormous columns of the enemy, chose his ground to fight, and, while waiting for General Longstreet, turned savagely, like a lion at bay—these movements undoubtedly reveal military genius of the first order, and vindicate the claim of the leader who executed them to the title of a great General.

Where the opposing forces are anything like equal, war is a contest of brains. It is the Generals who do the fighting, so to speak, and not the soldiers. If one

39

overcomes the other, and defeats or destroys his army, the inquirer will not have to go very far to discover the reason. One side is victor because the General was a better master of the art of making war than his opponent—because his plans were deeper, his insight into those of the enemy more penerating, his execution more rapid, or his nerve more steady and indomitable. As at chess—the opponents may start equal, without advantage on either side; but the brain of Morphy[7] will easily win the game. Advance another step: let us say that the armies, instead of equal, are greatly unequal—that humanly speaking, one is sure to be defeated by the other, unless some force sufficient to turn the balance be thrown into the scale against numbers.

Then the General who wins the day is a General indeed!

"These were soldiers indeed!" Jackson said at Cold Harbor, as he looked at the ditch and abbatis over which the Texans charged on the enemy's batteries, and took them, at the point of the bayonet. *"He was a soldier indeed!"* will be the verdict of history in summing up the career and character of the famous General Stonewall.

If what is said above of the elements of great generalship be true—as it *is* true—let Jackson be tried by it. The noble Sydney Johnston said that, after all, he

7. Paul Charles Morphy, the unparalleled chess genius of the mid-nineteenth century, was probably the most accomplished chess player in history.

agreed with the popular philosophy that success was the test of merit. If Jackson's career is subjected to that test, his merits, as a leader, will be established. No soldier of the war has been more uniformly successful in his undertakings. He has never failed to achieve his object from the day when, with 2600 men, he held in check 20,000 at Kernstown, and covered our withdrawal from Centreville, to the battles around Manassas in August last, when he accomplished his object, cut the enemy's communications, and fell back just far enough to draw their columns into the clutches of the reserve under Longstreet. This movement has been called the greatest of the war, and hazardous as it appeared, was completely successful. Such successes are not accidental. They are the tests of generalship, and the man who achieves them is a born warrior. Such undoubtedly, let it be repeated, is General Jackson. The old faded cap covers a brain which revolves deep thoughts—the penetrating eyes beneath cannot be deceived. The wiliest foe cannot outwit the plain, simple-looking personage; no feint or trick can mislead the clear judgment presiding serenely over the fiery soul. Indeed, the enemy who tries to undermine him, secretly, is apt to find a mine beneath *him*—which, almost before he knows of its existence, is sprung upon him. It is not too much to say that the victor of Port Republic is more than a match for all his foes combined, in strategy, and their best friends might advise them hereafter to

depend upon numbers and hard fighting, if they wish
to snatch laurels from Jackson.[8]

Will the advice be relished? Or the prospect seem
encouraging? Will "Commissary" Banks, or Fremont
of the "Woolly Horse," take hope from the announcement? Unfortunately, that very "last resort" of *hard
fighting* is the strong point of our General. If Jackson
is famous for anything at all, it is for an inborn and
ineradicable tendency to stubborn, unyielding com-
bat, against any odds. Of this there is no sort of
question. He has little of the fiery dash of Rupert,
at the head of his cavaliers—but the very bull-dog
pertinacity and iron nerve of Cromwell—sworn to
conquer or die. It is said that he was in favor of
advancing upon McClellan at Harrison's Landing; on
Burnside at Fredericksburg—that he is always in
favor of advancing. — To advance and fight is the
military philosophy of General Jackson—and to go on
fighting until the enemy are whipped. He is a "second

8. "It is no part of my design to present a critical analysis of Jackson's
military movements. This must sooner or later be done, but at present
the atmosphere is not clear of the battle smoke, and figures indistinctly.
The time will come when the campaigns of Jackson will become the study
of military men in the old world and the new—the masterly advances and
retreats of the Valley; the descent against McClellan; the expedition to
Pope's rear which terminated in the second battle of Manassas; and the
great flank movement at Chancellorsville, which has made the tangled
brakes of the Spottsylvania wilderness famous forever.

"Under the grave exterior, the reserved demeanor, the old faded cos-
tume . . . the penetrating student of human nature might discern 'one of
the immortals.' . . . His career covered but two years, and he lives only in
memory. But history cannot avoid her landmarks; the great proportions of
Stonewall Jackson will sooner or later be delineated." Cooke, "Southern
Generals in Outline," *New York Daily News,* October 24, 1865.

day man"—in favor of commencing early and winding up late, and on the next day beginning again with new ardor. One conspicuous weakness he has—the bayonet, when the enemy stand obstinately, and give him trouble; much more when they press him hard, and seek to destroy him by overwhelming weight—then he has recourse to his favorite weapon, his chosen mode of fighting.

"Press them with the bayonet!" is the brief, cool order; and unless they can withstand the Old Stonewall Brigade in a charge, all is over.

Such is the man whom President Lincoln doubts not he can "destroy." Here is the imperial announcement, directed to McDowell, and dated Washington, May 21, 1862:

"General Fremont has been ordered by telegraph to move from Franklin on Harrisonburg, *to relieve Gen. Banks, and capture or destroy Jackson's or Ewell's forces.* You are instructed, laying aside for the present, the movement on Richmond, to put twenty thousand men in motion at once for the Shenandoah, moving on the line, or in advance of the Manassas Gap Railroad. *Your object will be to capture the forces of Jackson and Ewell,* either in co-operation with Gen. Fremont, or in case of a want of supplies or transportation interferes with his movement, *it is believed that the force with which you move will be sufficient to accomplish the object alone.*"

And General Irwin McDowell, with a candor

which is honorable to his character, replied:

"The Executive's order has been received—is in process of execution. *This a crushing blow to us.*"

In the mad tragi-comedy of this crazy war, no document will furnish better food for jests than this grave announcement that *Frémont had been telegraphed to release Banks and destroy Jackson!* High life below stairs could no further go—or the spirit of elegant humor in the grave chief magistrate who dispatched this characteristic order.

To "destroy" General Stonewall Jackson has, up to this time, quite failed of success. Many enterprising Yankees have patented their inventions to entrap our General, and been given a trial—but they did not fulfill "public expectations." What a long, sad line of woful bankrupts! How sorrowful they look, on the farther bank of that Stygian river from which they never shall come back! Consider all the deep tragedy in the careers of these celebrated Yankee Generals! — the glad hopes which they indulged; the roseate dreams; the proud anticipation of entire success; and the welcoming plaudits of their joyful countrymen, when they came back home with the "job" accomplished, and the troublesome Stonewall defeated or "destroyed." Look first upon that picture of exalted hopes, all *coleur de rose,* and joy; then on that other sketch of the "warrior's return." — His return without Stonewall, and not even with his wagons! Without success of any sort—without prisoners, without troops, without hope, without credit,

44

without honor! All defeated, overthrown, and ground
to powder by the obstinate, the inexorable General
Stonewall!

Let us look at the great funeral procession of
whipped Generals—dead reputations—at the procession which has ever increased in numbers—at these
shades of departed hereoes: Patterson, Banks, Shields,
Fremont, McDowell, McClellan, Pope, Kearney,
Burnside—such are the *dii majores* only, the leaders
of the woful column. They one and all undertook
the difficult task of "destroying" the famous Stonewall;
and they every one failed in the undertaking. —
They advanced with the most magnificent trains of
supplies—it was only to have them captured. They
led to the encounter the best troops of the North-
land—it was only to have them put to rout. They
brought to the contest new uniforms and fresh new
names—it was only to have them tarnished, and
covered with the mud and opprobrium of disaster
and defeat. Banks promised to be victor—and turned
out only "Commissary." Pope had "seen only the
backs" of Southerners, he said—but their faces were
revealed to his longing gaze at Slaughter mountain,
and he never wished to see them any more. He has
gone to contend with the Dacotahs in the West; and
General Banks to make war on women in New
Orleans. General Stonewall remains entirely un-
moved, and awaits the new crop of celebrated inven-
tors who have discovered the art of destroying him.

At his back are the heroes of the Old Brigade. They

are chatting by the camp-fire yonder not far distant from me—and recalling, it may be, the great scenes through which they have passed. On the Shenandoah, the Chickahominy, the James, the Rapidan, the Rappahannock, Bull Run, and the Potomac—on the banks of these rivers, in the mountains and the lowlands, they have played such a world-famous part! Do they remember now all those weary marches, the hard battles, the desperate charges, the lost comrades? Believe me, one of the saddest phases of war is that memory of the good companions dead and gone: — and in the Old Brigade there are many to mourn. I think, as I write, of the gallant boy who fell yonder at Manassas—the "little corporal" of the valiant company—who fell as he was cheering his comrades on, and whose life-blood gushed over a miniature in his bosom, and stained the blue velvet case with its crimson. I mourn for him yet, as a fair girl mourns —as many are mourning for their dear dead loves; their sons, their brothers, and their husbands, or their sweethearts—fallen on the field of honor from the ranks of the Old Brigade.

The graves of its heroic souls are on the weird plains of Manassas, under the shadow of the Blue Ridge, in the marshes of the Chickahominy—wherever it has fought almost. At Groveton the survivors fought over those very graves of their dead brethren. A General, three Colonels, many officers and privates I recall who sleep their last sleep. Virginia received in her capitol, and buried, near the ashes of Monroe, in Hollywood, one of the bravest of these dead ones—General Charles Winder; and I saw by the hearse Admiral Buchanan, who fought the Merrimac—fit mourner for the leader of the Old Stonewall Brigade.

In speaking of this noble and heroic band I have said nothing, I believe, which the popular heart will not echo. It has marched to glory through the fires of battle, and achieved its aim. Its memory, and that of its commander, can never die.

The General and his Old Legion are resting yonder, but the struggle is not ended, and the sky is still dark with clouds. They talk around the camp-fire now, amid the pines, but will spring to arms again, ere long, when they hear the "Fall in!" of their chief.

At their head is the officer with the faded uniform—and the cheer which greets him, tells him plainly that the Old Stonewall Brigade is ready to follow wherever he leads.

Heroic souls! worthy of that great heroic chief! He who writes these lines salutes you from his heart of hearts, and wishes you, each and all, every blessing. Worthy children of Virginia, and sons of the great South! — the time will soon come now, when your marches will be ended, when the musket will be laid aside, and the tragic drama of this bitter struggle will terminate in liberty and peace.

When that day shall arrive, as arrive it will, ere long, there are many who will envy you the power to say

"I fought under Jackson in the Old Stonewall Brigade!"

Cooke's Lives of Jackson

JOHN ESTEN COOKE'S *Stonewall Jackson and the Old Stonewall Brigade* stands alone as a Confederate view of "Old Jack" and his "foot cavalry." Virtually unknown in 1861, Jackson was destined to "live in song and story as the popular hero of the war." His untimely death after the battle of Chancellorsville in May 1863 brought forth verses to his memory in nearly every paper in the South. Not only in the Confederacy but also in London and even at the North, biographers hastened to prepare books about the dead hero. But Cooke's series of articles is the only noteworthy account written during the life of the General.

During the winter of 1862-'63 Captain Esten Cooke was ordnance officer and aide-de-camp at "Camp No-Camp," General J. E. B. Stuart's headquarters in Northern Virginia during the "mire truce" of bad weather. One of the most promising younger literary men during the years immediately before the War, Cooke could not restrain himself from putting his observations of army life on paper. In January 1863 he became a correspondent of *The Southern Illustrated News*, a lively weekly established in Richmond the previous September. His first contribution to the *News*, "The Song of the Rebel," was published in its

49

issue for January 24, 1863. Two issues later, publication of his "Outlines from the Outpost" began.[1]

"Outlines from the Outpost" catches the spirit of Confederate camp life more fully than any of Cooke's later writing. Much of the material was used again in his *Wearing of the Gray*, New York, 1867, but after the War it had to be toned down, and the freshness of Cooke's pieces for a wholly Confederate audience was often lost. Many of the incidents are incorporated into *Surry of Eagle's-Nest*, New York, 1866, but the reality is obscured by the fiction. In the "Outlines" as they were originally written, the reader is rewarded with a perception of Confederate camp life that can be found nowhere else. And the installments on "Stonewall Jackson, and the Old Stonewall Brigade" are the best of the "Outlines." When other material was reworked, these chapters were largely ignored, as Cooke had by then written a more extended biography of Jackson.[2] Thus, they are here reprinted for the first time just as Cooke wrote them for Confederate readers, reprinted with all the dash and passion and hero worship that marked Cooke's wartime reporting.

"I have read with interest the heroic actions of the *Stonewall Brigade*," wrote a Confederate soldier from the lines at Fredericksburg, "and I see no reason why the Army of the Potomac, except the *Stonewall*

1. The articles appeared at intervals until October 10, 1863. The sketches entitled "Stonewall Jackson, and the Old Stonewall Brigade" are in volume I, numbers 22-24, February 7, 14, and 21, 1863. (Each issue was predated one week; thus the issue for February 7 was distributed January 31.)

2. For full bibliographical descriptions of Cooke's and other nearly contemporary biographies of Jackson, see "The Chief Early Biographies of Jackson," p. 67-72.

Brigade, should not be disbanded and sent home, and leave that *immortal Brigade* which has done all the fighting to crown themselves with immortality, by ending the war alone."[3]

This sarcasm, directed February 4, 1863, to the editors of *The Southern Illustrated News*, was inspired by the first of Cooke's articles on Jackson. But neither this letter from "Rip" nor another signed "A Volunteer" which reads in part "he says the Stone Wall brigade dose all the fiting and never stragels   the solgers is hard down on that artical   tell the Riter for God Sak to Stop it"[4] persuaded the editors to halt the series of intimate glimpses of the Army of Northern Virginia that was proving highly popular with their readers.

"Leave me, O 'Volunteer' and 'Rip,' " answered Cooke, "my fondness and admiration for that 'old tattered, ball-pierced flag' of the brigade . . . — the old ensign which so many of my friends have died under, pouring out their blood for the sacred liberties of the South. Those names ever dear to me—those forms which now sleep the sleep of glory—are inseparably connected with the Old Brigade, and I am jealous of whatever affects their memories. They made it what it was—gave it its great fame—and I would rather have my critics say 'His praise is extravagant!' than 'He tried to dim the glories of the Old Brigade!' "[5]

A veteran of the first battle at Manassas and a member of Stuart's staff since the spring of 1862, Cooke

3. [John Esten Cooke,] "Outlines from the Outpost," *The Southern Illustrated News*, October 10, 1863, II, 107.
4. *Ibid.*
5. *Ibid.*

had been in the principal campaigns of the Army of Northern Virginia. But his heart was not in the military life. His most memorable wartime service lies in his record of events and characters in the daily life of the Confederate army.

"Such personal details of the characters of these eminent men will not be uninteresting," he later wrote, "to the lovers of noble natures of whatever 'faction;' nor is the fondness for such particulars either trivial or ignoble. They elucidate biography and history—which are the same—for they present the likeness of the actor in the drama, his character and endowments—and to know what great men *are*, is better than to know what they *perform*. What Lee, Jackson, Johnston, Stuart, and their associates accomplished, history will record; how they looked, and moved, and spoke, will attract much less attention from the 'historian of the future.' The august muse of history will make her partial and passionate, or fair and dignified, summary of the events of the late war . . . and mete out in rounded periods what she thinks the due amount of glory or shame to the actors, in gray or in blue. But meanwhile the real personages disappear, and the colours fade, figures become historical personages, not men. And events, too, 'suffer change.' They are fused in the mass; generalization replaces the particular incident as it does the impressive trait;—the terrible dust of 'official documents' obscures personages, characters, and events."[6]

"Stonewall Jackson, and the Old Stonewall Brigade" is Cooke's account of the Hero of the Valley, his men,

6. Cooke, *Wearing of the Gray*, New York, 1867, p. [xiii]-xiv.

and his campaigns before the "terrible dust" had settled. In it Cooke caught the feeling of the Army of Northern Virginia, the feeling of indefatigable soldiers determined to follow an inspired leader wherever the fortunes of an inexorable war should take them. In it he caught

> . . . The man of *Kernstown*—
> Of all that great campaign
> Far off in the snowy *Valley*
> Where he met with grand disdain,
> The plundering Yankee cohorts
> By *Shields* and *Fremont* led
> To the field of *Port Republic*—
> To sleep in a gory bed!
>
> How he fell from the mountain passes
> Like a hawk upon his prey,
> And the great host of *McClellan*
> Like a vapor passed away:
> How charging at *Cold Harbour*
> He swept them from his path,
> As the dry leaves of the forest
> Are swept by the tempest's wrath.
> So a health to *Stonewall Jackson!*
>
> That soul so brave and true,
> That never a taint of craven guile
> Or shade of falsehood knew!—
> Who never shrunk from foeman's steel
> In the heart of the deadliest fight,
> And bears on his radiant banner's fold
> "May God defend the Right!"[7]

7. [Cooke,] "The Song of the Rebel," *The Southern Illustrated News*, I, January 24, 1863, 5.

These sketches of "Stonewall Jackson, and the Old Stonewall Brigade" form the first of four biographical treatments of General Jackson by Cooke. The second treatment, a full-length military biography, was published in Richmond later in 1863. The third was prepared as a new edition for Confederate or English publication but never appeared. And the fourth was published by D. Appleton & Company, New York, in 1866 and reissued in 1876 with the addition of an elaborate appendix.

The Southern Illustrated News for May 23, 1863, (published May 16), which editorially memorialized Jackson, announced, "In press, and will shortly be issued, the Life of Stonewall Jackson, the Hero of the Present War for Independence!" This was the first public word of the forthcoming volume by Cooke. It roused the ire of the *Central Presbyterian*, the partisan of Robert Lewis Dabney, who had been authorized by the General's family to prepare a life of Jackson. The *Central Presbyterian* condemned the project of Ayres & Wade, publishers of the *News*, as unauthorized and attacked Cooke (without calling his name) as a "self-appointed upstart" and "a literary and . . . social impostor." Its editor wrote:

> . . . [I]t is a painful fact that hardly had the remains of General Jackson reached their quiet resting place in his beloved Valley, before his family and friends were surprised and grieved to find an ostentatious announcement from a certain printing office in this city that *they* would prepare and issue forthwith a volume

containing the history of his *life*. Who asked this at their hands? Can they explain how, in any way recognized as decent under the principles which regulate refined society, they come to be the vehicle by which the public, sorrowing as never before since the death of Washington, is to receive its first history of the great and good General Jackson.[8]

In defending themselves, Ayres & Wade said: "We had determined four months before the death of General Jackson, to publish his memoirs in popular form ... The death of General Jackson neither advanced or delayed the publication an hour."[9] Cooke kept a diary during the spring of 1863, and there is no evidence in it to support the claim of Ayres & Wade that he was engaged on the biography before Jackson's death,[10] but the further argument of their case by Ayres & Wade is a good testimonial for the value of a biography written by their correspondent:

We entrusted the materials we had collected to Major John Esten Cooke. We selected Mr. Cooke for a variety of reasons. He stood high in the literary world. He had already been the

8. The article from the *Central Presbyterian* was reprinted in full in the *Daily Richmond Examiner*, June 19, 1863, and in *The Southern Illustrated News*, July 4, 1863, II, 4.
9. *The Southern Illustrated News*, July 4, 1863, II, 4.
10. Cooke's earliest reference to the project is the following undated entry in his diary, written some time after May 12, 1863: "I have been incessantly engaged on the 'Life of Stonewall Jackson' having in about a week or ten days, got him through the Battle of Cedar Run. Rarely have I worked so hard—and it has been done in the midst of a thousand distractions." Cooke MSS, Duke University Library.

author of many works. He was a man of irreproachable character, and had led a laborious life from his boyhood. Holding a position upon the staff of Gen. Jeb. Stuart, he was enabled to watch and carefully study the movements of Gen. Jackson. This last circumstance we thought a matter of considerable importance. Everybody can tell, in the twinkling of an eye, the vast difference between the narrative of a person who has seen what he describes, and that of a person who obtains his knowledge at second hand. Major Cooke, moreover, is a master of a lively style, excels in description, and was in every way the proper person to produce a lively, popular history of the great warrior."[11]

Cooke himself, in a note "To the Reader" in his *Jackson*, graciously acknowledged the projected biography by Dr. Dabney and characterized its author as "a friend of the deceased leader, and especially competent to describe the religious phase of his character." He declared that "No one will look for that volume with greater interest, or read it with more unalloyed pleasure, than the writer of the present sketch."[12]

But the controversy stirred up by the *Central Presbyterian* was really beside the point—except as good advertising. Neither Cooke's nor Dabney's was to be the first biography of the General. The delays of Confederate publishing deferred the issue of Cooke's book until August 15, and the biography by Dabney was never published in the Confederacy but appeared

11. *The Southern Illustrated News*, July 4, 1863, II, 4.
12. [Cooke,] *The Life of Stonewall Jackson*, Richmond, 1863, p.iv.

in London in two volumes in 1864 and 1866. In the meantime the first biography of Jackson had been brought out at Augusta, Georgia, in June, and the General had been memorialized in a pamphlet issue of H. M. Thompson's poem *The Death of Jackson*[13] published in the same city. This first biography was a slight affair put together by Charles Hallock. Its principal claim to interest is its undoubted priority as a life of Jackson. Although not entered for copyright in the Southern District Court of Georgia until June 13,[14] it was reviewed as early as June 6 by *The Southern Field and Fireside*, which reported: "It is a most acceptable memorial of the life of this great and good man, and is admirably adapted for circulation in camp, where it will be sought after with avidity."[15]

When Cooke's book did appear it was an immediate success. The publishers reported three thousand copies sold the first day.[16] It was soon printed in New York in a pirated edition[17] issued by Charles B. Rich-

13. H. M. Thompson, *The Death of Jackson*, by H. M. Thompson. Augusta[,] Ga[.]: Constitutionalist Steam Press. 1863. cover-title, 7 p.

14. ALS, C. S. Henry, Clerk of the District Court, Southern District of Georgia, Savannah, to Judah P. Benjamin, November 13, 1863. Pickett papers, folio 116, Manuscripts Division, Library of Congress.

15. *The Southern Field and Fireside* (Augusta), June 6, 1863, n. s., I, 151.

16. *The Southern Illustrated News*, September 5, 1863, II, 68.

17. *The Southern Illustrated News* for November 21, 1863, noted "that the Yankees have republished, without 'leave or license,' 'The Life of Stonewall Jackson,' written by Major John Esten Cooke, and published by the proprietors of this paper." It quoted from the notice of the New York *World*: "'The heated passions of the combatants must have time to subside, both at the North and the South, before the life of "Stonewall Jackson" can be written as it should be. In the meantime we must take such a record of him as we can get—a volume like this, for instance, written from the extreme Southern point of view and for the Southern people.' "

ardson. Another unauthorized issue was brought out in London. In both these editions the authorship is credited to "Daniels of Richmond;" *i.e.*, John Moncure Daniel, the Richmond editor. But what was perhaps the highest compliment for Cooke's book came in an inverted manner, in a Federal Army order interdicting its sale:

> In obedience to orders from headquarters Department of the Ohio, the circulation of a book entitled "Life, services and campaign of Stonewall Jackson, from official papers, contemporary narratives and acquaintance, by a Virginian," is interdicted within the limits of this command, and the publication and circulation of all other books of a similar character, put forth for similar purposes, are likewise interdicted.
>
> The object of such books is not to afford the people correct information regarding the history of the rebellion and its leaders, but [they] are put forth by the traitors themselves, and republished in the loyal States for the purpose of stirring up discontent and sedition, and encouraging treasonable practices and treasonable conversation by representing the crime of treason in false and alluring colors, and should no more be tolerated than an emissary sent direct by the revolted States to advocate the justice of the rebellion publicly before the people. Any one found with copies of such books in his possession, offering or intending to offer them for sale,

is either a traitor or one who loves money better than his country, and his right to the book is declared forfeited, and the same is ordered to be seized and destroyed.[18]

The year 1863 also saw the publication of biographies of Jackson[19] by Miss Catherine Cooper Hopley, an Englishwoman who had lived in the South immediately before and during the first part of the War; by James D. McCabe, jr., a young Richmond writer; and by Markinfield Addey, apparently the unidentified

18. U. S. War department, *The War of the Rebellion, a Compilation of the Official Records of the Union and Confederate Armies*, Ser. I, vol. XXXIX, pt. 2, Washington, 1892, p.7.

19. The major contemporary works about Jackson have been mentioned and are fully described in the section "The Chief Early Biographies of Jackson." These, however, were not all. Dr. Dabney's *True Courage: A Discourse Commemorative of Lieut. General Thomas J. Jackson* was published in two editions in 1863 at Richmond by the Presbyterian Committee of Publication of the Confederate States. The Board of Visitors of the Virginia Military Institute ordered the printing of Superintendent Francis Henney Smith's *Discourse on the Life and Character of Lt. Gen. Thos. J. Jackson, (C. S. A.) Late Professor of Natural and Experimental Philosophy in the Virginia Military Institute.* This speech was read before the Board July 1, 1863, and, with the proceedings of the Institute in honor of Jackson, was printed later in the same year by Ritchie & Dunnavant at Richmond. Some time after June 24 James Beverlin Ramsey's sermon *True Eminence Founded on Holiness. A Discourse Occasioned by the Death of Lieut. Gen. T. J. Jackson. Preached in the First Presbyterian Church of Lynchburg, May 24th, 1863* was printed in Lynchburg by the Virginian "Water-Power Presses Print."

An anonymous pamphlet biography (fifteen pages only) appeared in England with the imprint of Bacon & Co., London, 1863, as *Life and Military Career of "Stonewall" Jackson.* There was even a juvenile about him, Edward M. Boykin's unsigned *The Boys and Girls Stories of the War,* Richmond, [1863?]. At least eleven pieces of Confederate sheet music were inspired by the General. Most interesting of these are John Williamson Palmer's "Stonewall Jackson's Way" and the song "My Wife and Child" published by an enterprising Richmond firm (George Dunn & Company) as with "poetry by the late lamented hero, General 'Stonewall' Jackson." This poem had been written years before by Henry Rootes Jackson.

pseudonym of a New York hack writer. But Cooke's work was by far the best of the early accounts of Jackson's career. It cannot claim the accolade belonging to a really distinguished biography, but it can justly claim to have derived from actual observation and has, therefore, lasting value.

Cooke himself recognized the faults of the volume. "The work has been written under disadvantages," he said, "which entitle it to the liberal criticism of the reader. It was undertaken without thought of the probable activity of the summer campaign [the movement into Pennsylvania that led to Confederate defeat at Gettysburg], and has been composed in bivouac—by the road-side—immediately before and after engagements—amid scenes and under circumstances which have rendered deliberate writing impossible."[20]

The unprecedented eagerness with which the public sought copies of the publication determined Cooke to rework his manuscript for a second edition. Only four days after the publication of *The Life of Stonewall Jackson* he wrote Captain Jed Hotchkiss, topographical engineer of Jackson's staff:

> *Headqrs. Cav. Div*
> *Captain:* *Aug 19. 1863*
> *I have directed the publishers of the "Life of Stonewall Jackson" (whose paternity—that of the* life *not the publishers, you have no doubt guessed) to send you a copy of the first printed.*
> *I wish you to do me and literature a favor: I mean, to read the book, and correct all the*

20. [Cooke,] *The Life of Stonewall Jackson*, p.[iii].

*errors you find, and send me the mem^a. This
will give you some trouble, but I know that you
revere the memory of your great Chief, and are
anxious to have his 'record' properly placed
before the world.*

*Please make all the corrections you can—slash
me as roughly as you choose—and give me any
additional material you can spare. You ought
to write a life of Jackson yourself and I have
no doubt you will—and I don't wish to trespass
on your ground.*[21] *But you might spare me a
few items. They will be "thankfully received"—
and your name among the authorities relied on,
to be referred to in a second edition, would
give additional strength to the book, from your
long and intimate knowledge, especially of the
Valley campaign.*

*Let me hear from you by courier, thro' Gen.
Lee's Headqrs.*

*Yours very truly
Jno. Esten Cooke
Capt. &c*

*Capt. J. Hotchkiss
Gen Ewell's Staff*[22]

Captain Hotchkiss's copy of the *Jackson* is now in
the McGregor Library at the University of Virginia.
Its markings show that Hotchkiss used Cooke's volume
in the preparation of his *The Battle-Fields of Virginia.*

21. In 1867 the D. Van Nostrand Company of New York published Hotchkiss's *The Battle-Fields of Virginia, Chancellorsville; Embracing the Opera-
tions from the First Battle of Fredericksburg to the Death of Lieutenant-
General Jackson.*
22. ALS laid in the McGregor Library copy of *The Life of Stonewall
Jackson.*

General W. N. Pendleton is given as the authority for many of the manuscript notes, and it was also on Pendleton that Cooke apparently relied for help in the preparation of his revision of the *Jackson*. Work on the revision was under way by fall. On October 5, 1863, he noted "Revolving my life of Jackson, second edition, but the weather is so delightful, it is hard to get at it." On March 9, 1864, he recorded in his diary: "Today I finished the battles around Richmond in Jackson and when Gen. Pendleton's notes come, will finish up Manassas."[23]

Cooke was a rapid writer, but he was expending both his time and talents on this labor of love. "The work has taken me a good while," he wrote April 10, 1864, "having been commenced in November—the last part—and occasionally driven ahead. It is incomparably better than the first edition and will give me some reputation I think." The next day, he could rejoice that his manuscript was complete: "This very moment at about 9 P. M. on the 11th of April in the year 1864 (date to be handed down to the remotest posterity) I have finished 'Jackson!!!' It makes some 1182 pp. but as the old text—also marked, unpaged— is scattered through it, it will make nearer 13, or 1400 pages of my MS.—easy 700 pages of letter size. Now that will make nearly as many printed pages   800 and thick will be the size of the work if Providence permits it to be printed."

23. The quotations concerning the proposed second edition of the *Jackson* are from Cooke's diary, whose MS. volumes have been dispersed. The 1863 quotation is from the part now in the private library of Mr. C. Waller Barrett; the others are from parts now at Duke University.

Providence did not permit. Cooke was obviously pleased with the job he had done. But by 1864 shortages were curtailing publishing in Richmond. It would be greatly to his advantage to publish in London. His diary entry for May 29, 1864, reflected his plans and hopes: "Made arrangements to have 'Jackson' copied by Nannie Steger, and Mr. Benjamin very politely promised to forward the MS. to London. I am having maps made, and it will bring me, I hope, at least £500 which is $50000 or $10,000 worth of *land*." But the good offices of the Confederate State Department could not assure the safe passage of the manuscript through the ever-tightening blockade. The manuscript did not reach London. Although Cooke retained a copy, which escaped destruction during the burning of Richmond by being buried, this revision was not suitable for publication in a reunited country, and this third biographical treatment of Jackson—the one which Cooke believed his best—was never printed.[24]

The Virginian, however, set to work on another complete revision of his *Jackson*, published by D. Appleton & Company in 1866. Relieved of many of the opprobrious epithets cast at the Federals in earlier versions and corrected by the incorporation of General Pendleton's notes, it nevertheless lacks the militant spark that makes the first edition delightful reading. Not for a generation would a really distinguished biography come from the pen of Englishman G. F. R. Henderson.[25] But Cooke had contributed to Confed-

24. John O. Beaty, *John Esten Cooke, Virginian*, New York, 1922, p.89-90. If the manuscript has survived, the present editor does not know where it is.
25. George Francis Robert Henderson, *Stonewall Jackson and the American Civil War*...London, New York [etc.], Longmans, Green and Co., 1898. 2 vols.

erate historiography in his, the first adequate description of Jackson.

"Stonewall Jackson, and the Old Stonewall Brigade" is not a précis of the full length biography. But in this short piece, the precursor of all later biographies of the General, is caught, in the colorful phraseology and heroic periods of the time, the living spirit of the "Blue Light Elder" and his army of the Valley of Virginia. Both among the writings by Cooke and the writings about Jackson it stands alone as the livest and freshest of all.

A Note on the Illustrations

THE frontispiece is reproduced from the Mc-
Gregor Library copy of *The Life of Stonewall
Jackson*, Richmond, 1863. It is a lithograph by
Ernest Crehen, chief Richmond lithographer of the
war period. The *News* told the story of the portrait
in its issue for July 11, 1863:

> We are informed that some of our good
> friends (?) have insinuated that the picture of
> Gen. Jackson, which we have announced to
> accompany our Book is not a *bona fide* likeness
> of the late lamented hero. To relieve all doubt
> in regard to this matter, we beg to announce
> that the picture was taken for us by Mr. D. T.
> Cowell, of the Minnis Galle[r]y. Through the
> kindness of a friend we were enabled to procure
> for Mr. Cowell a letter of introduction to Gen.
> Jackson, who, immediately upon the arrival of
> the artist at his headquarters at Fredericksburg,
> consented to sit for the picture. Three different
> photographs were taken at the time, one of
> which was spoiled by the shaking of the instru-
> ment. Of the other two, it is needless for us to
> speak. *The habitues* of the Minnis Gallery know
> full well the style of pictures taken at that first
> class establishment. The three negatives are
> now in possession of Mr. Cowell, who will

immediately after the publication of our Book, furnish all who wish photographs for the purpose of framing, with a copy of the only life-like picture of the distinguished General now in existence. With the picture, further than the publication of our forthcoming volume, we have nothing to do. All applications should be made to Messrs. Minnis & Cowell.

The lithograph was issued separately as well as in the book.

The portrait on the dust jacket appeared on the front wrapper of the first edition of *The Life of Jackson*. It was engraved by Hurdle, an engraver for Ayres & Wade and their *Southern Illustrated News*, and was used also as an illustration for a long article about Cooke's book in the issue of the *News* for August 29, 1863.

The pencil drawing of Jackson is inserted in the McGregor Library copy of the life and is labeled: "Gen. T. J. Jackson considering dispatches—at the Old Church near Mechanicsville   Louisa Co.   Va— Tuesday July 29th 1862 Drawn by Hon   A. R. Boteler." It is reproduced here facing page 16.

The Chief Early
Biographies of Jackson

1. MARKINFIELD ADDEY, *"Stonewall Jackson." The Life and Military Career of Thomas Jonathan Jackson, Lieutenant General in the Confederate Army.* By Markinfield Addey . . . New-York: C. T. Evans [etc., etc.] 1863. 240 p., front. (port.)

With slight changes the same text was published anonymously the next year by John Bradburn as *"Old Jack" and His Foot Cavalry; or, A Virginian Boy's Progress to Renown.* In 1866 it was reissued by M. Doolady under the title *Life and Military Career of Thomas Jonathan Jackson, Lieutenant-General in the Confederate Army* as the second part of the anonymous *Life and Imprisonment of Jefferson Davis, Together With the Life and Military Career of Stonewall Jackson.*

The Richmond Whig for July 8, 1863, carried an editorial based on a Northern announcement of Addey's book. The announcement had promised an introduction by the Rev. George Junkin, the father of General Jackson's first wife and, until he removed to the North at the beginning of the war, President of Washington College.

"This is the Yankee announcement," wrote the *Whig*, "of a nice Yankee job and speculation in Jackson's remains. The book, however slovenly executed, will be sure to accomplish all that its Yankee authors expect—it will pay. Who 'Mr. Markinfield Addey' may be, is a matter of conjecture purely, for his name is entirely new to the world of letters. With the Rev. George Junkin, we are better acquainted. He was, for a number of years, the President of Washington College, an abolitionist at heart if not avowedly, and a conceited irrascible and troublesome old hypocrite, who kept himself and everybody around him continually in hot water. General Jackson's first wife was his daughter. Long previous to the war which made Jackson immortal and consigned him to a premature grave, his reverend father in law ceased to be on good terms with him, and the two had ceased even to speak to each other. This is the person who takes upon himself the solemn and remunerative duty of portraying the social and religious life of one of the purest and bravest men that ever lived, and, for the sake of gain, will devote himself to the genial task of enumerating the imaginary influences which led Stonewall Jackson to espouse the Southern cause.

"Mr. Markinfield Addey will, we are quite sure, record Jackson's military career with an affluence of praise which will be in as bad taste as his narrative, in the main, will be false. But the Reverend father in law, whetting his vulturous beak against the clasp of his empty port monnaie, will befoul the memory of the illustrious deceased with the slaver of pharasaical pity [piety?] which the rancour of personal enmity has rendered at once venomous and putrescent. That Junkin or any other Yankee should be capable of comprehend-

68

ing, much less appreciating, the influences which in-
duced a noble spirit like Stonewall Jackson to take up
arms in behalf of the just cause is simply impossible.
Junkin's introduction must, of necessity, be a slander.
But it will put money in his purse, and beyond that,
no genuine Yankee ever aspires."

The short preface to Addey's book is unsigned but
is along the lines promised by Dr. Junkin. It is a re-
strained and dignified tribute to "one who was so
noble in heart and so chivalric in action."

2. [JOHN ESTEN COOKE,] *The Life of Stonewall Jackson. From Official Papers, Cotemporary Narratives,
and Personal Acquaintance*. By a Virginian . . . Richmond: Ayres & Wade. Illustrated News Steam Presses.
1863. 305 p. front. (port.)

A pirated edition was issued in New York in the
same year as "Reprinted from advance sheets of the
Richmond edition." It was published by Charles B.
Richardson who credited the authorship to John Moncure Daniel, the Richmond editor, by stamping on
the spine: "Daniels of Richmond." This edition used
two portraits of Jackson as illustrations. In the title the
word "cotemporary" was changed to "contemporary."
A London issue differs from the New York edition
only in adding "Bacon & Co., Sampson Low, Son &
Co." and their address in the imprint.

3. JOHN ESTEN COOKE, *Stonewall Jackson: A Military
Biography* . . . By John Esten Cooke. New York: D.
Appleton and Company, 1866. 470 p. front. (port.),
maps (1 fold.)

Reissued in 1876 in an edition expanded to 587 pages by the addition of "an appendix, containing personal reminiscences, and a full account of the ceremonies attending the unveiling of Foley's statue, including the oration by Moses D. Hoge, D.D., by Rev. J. Wm. Jones."

4. ROBERT LEWIS DABNEY, *Life of Lieut — Gen. Thomas J. Jackson (Stonewall Jackson)*, by Professor R. L. Dabney . . . Edited by Rev. W. Chalmers . . . London: J. Nisbet & Co., 1864-66. 2 v. front. (port.)

This was republished in New York by Blelock & Co. in 1866 in a single volume of 742 pages. The title page and a few loose pages of a Confederate printing are at the Duke University Library. Apparently work on a Confederate edition was begun in 1865 by W. W. Holden at Raleigh, North Carolina, printing for Sterling, Campbell and Albright, Greensboro publishers, but the work was not completed.

5. [CHARLES HALLOCK,] *A Complete Biographical Sketch of "Stonewall" Jackson: Giving a Full and Accurate Account of the Leading Events of His Military Career, His Dying Moments, and the Obsequies at Richmond and Lexington.* Augusta, Ga.: Steam Power-Press Chronicle and Sentinel. 1863. 38, [1], ii p.

Hallock's biography of Jackson was reprinted in both Halifax and Montreal in 1863. In the preface to the Halifax edition he wrote: "It was first published in the Confederate States, at Augusta, Georgia, where it found a sale of 5000 copies in a few weeks. It was put to press within eighteen days after the death of

Jackson, and is the first biography of the General ever published."

6. [CATHERINE COOPER HOPLEY,] *"Stonewall" Jackson, Late General of the Confederate States Army. A Biographical Sketch, and an Outline of His Virginian Campaigns.* By the Author of "Life in the South." London: Chapman and Hall, 1863. xiv, 178 p., fold. map.

"Those circumstances which caused the author to be a resident of Va., during the greater portion of the time in which the following events took place, enabled her to watch the incidents as they were brought home by the actors of the drama; incidents of the wars, and of their effect upon society, especially as regards the blockade; which latter circumstance gives a colouring to this great and terrible civil war, that tinges every event of the social life of the Southerner. . . .

"The author now ventures to arrange in the form of a narrative, as much as is within the province of a woman to describe, without wishing to intrude beyond that limit. Such facts as have been collected, and are here introduced, together with dates and topography, will at the present time be found useful, until a more efficient pen shall do justice to one of the noblest characters in history." p. vi-vii.

7. [JAMES DABNEY MCCABE,] *The Life of Lieut. Gen. T. J. Jackson.* By an Ex-Cadet. Richmond, Va.: Printed and Published by James E. Goode. 1863. 128 p.

A second edition, "revised and enlarged by the author" to 196 pages, was published by Goode in 1864.

71

In his preface to the first edition McCabe wrote: "The book was complete and put in press on the 29th day of May, but the failure to procure paper, and other difficulties hard to overcome, have prevented its appearance at an earlier period." The biography was not published until late October 1863.

INDEX

73

74

C O L O P H O N

Linotype setting by Jerry Grizzle and Mark Rinker;
makeup by Joe Poindexter and Mark Rinker; presswork
by William R. Travis; collotype illustrations by Meriden
Gravure of Connecticut; binding by the Bohn Company of New York. Twenty-six hundred copies printed
at the University of Virginia Press in August 1954.

4,000